TO:

FROM:

Published by Hallmark Gift Books,
a division of Hallmark Cards, Inc.,
Kansas City, MO 64141
Visit us on the Web at Hallmark.com.

Editor: Emily Osborn
Art Director: Kevin Swanson
Designer: Mark Voss
Production Designer: Bryan Ring

ISBN: 978-1-59530-293-9

BOK2109

Printed and bound in China

NOW YOU'RE 60!

BY BRANDON CROSE

Hallmark

America's "TV Generation" has seen the most dramatic changes in politics and culture of any generation before or since. You were raised in a time of growth, prosperity, and the very real threat of nuclear annihilation. You came of age amidst war, protest, and revolutionary music. You remember a time before personal computers, where you were when J.F.K. was shot, and your first color television. (You may be trying to forget the Disco Era, but you were there for that, too.) Most significantly, your story is also the story of how much America has changed since World War II. And it wasn't all Woodstock...

WHEN YOU WERE
BORN

IN THE NEWS

Having lived through (and possibly fought in) World War II, your parents watched as the less popular Korean War claimed 36,940 American and 3.9 million Korean lives.

It was a time of prosperity and material comfort, but the Red Scare was in full effect: Ethel and Julius Rosenberg were sentenced to death by electric chair for sharing U.S. nuclear secrets with the Soviet Union. (Ethel's brother was the prosecution's chief witness.)

Senator Joseph McCarthy's wild accusations of Communist sympathizers and spies within the federal government further amplified Cold War fear… until the Army–McCarthy hearings led to his fall from grace.

7 million people attended New York City ticker tape parade for General MacArthur

EVENTS

· ·

Established manufacturers didn't think that Marion Donovan's "disposable diaper" would sell. (Pampers didn't capitalize on the idea until years after you were out of diapers.) Thank goodness most American families owned washing machines!

Your father may have purchased a new home movie camera, such as the Bell & Howell Sportster, to record your first steps. It retailed for $99.75. (Not such a great deal if you consider that the average salary was just over $3,000.)

Two-thirds of American homes had a telephone, and AT&T had just introduced direct-dial coast-to-coast telephone service. The first call was from New Jersey to California, which took eighteen seconds to connect.

The first commercial computer, the UNIVAC I (UNIVersal Automatic Computer), had just hit "shelves"—but at 14x7x9 feet, it took up most of a room.

MUSIC

You may not remember now, but "Doggie in the Window" by Patti Page, "I Saw Mommy Kissing Santa Claus" by Jimmy Boyd, and "Papa Loves Mambo" by Perry Como were among the first songs you ever heard.

There's a strong chance that your parents also enjoyed Jackie Gleason's first album, *Music for Lovers Only*—it remained on the Top Ten charts for a record 153 weeks.

The music that shaped your teen years was born when you were—a Cleveland, Ohio, disc jockey first coined the term "rock 'n' roll" to make rhythm and blues music more palatable to a young white audience.

MOVIES

. . . .

Your parents may have taken an evening to see *A Streetcar Named Desire*, starring a young (and muscled) Marlon Brando. It was nominated for twelve Academy Awards and won four of them, losing "Best Actor" to Humphrey Bogart in *The African Queen*.

Cold War fear of world annihilation found its way into many movies of the time, but none so explicitly as in science fiction hit *The Day the Earth Stood Still.*

Walt Disney also released his now–classic animated feature *Alice In Wonderland*, but it was not popular until the 1970s, when it found an unexpected second life for its "trippy" psychedelic sequences.

TV

Many families enjoyed their convenient and modern TV dinners on folding TV tables while watching shows such as *I Love Lucy, The Jack Benny Show, Fireside Theatre,* and *The Colgate Comedy Hour.*

Your generation's "Man of Steel" was not Christopher Reeve, but George Reeves, in *Adventures of Superman.* His costume was brown and grey until the show was later broadcast in color.

More than 4.4 million families owned a television set, and thousands more were buying one each day. Television's "Golden Age" had begun.

Sid Caesar's *Your Show of Shows* launched the careers of a few familiar writers: Neil Simon, Mel Brooks, and Woody Allen.

Mr. Potato Head was the first toy advertised on television. The Hasbro toy raked in over $4 million during its first year.

SPORTS

Willie Mays, "The Say Hey Kid," made his Major League Baseball debut with the New York Giants, and was awarded National League Rookie of the Year.

Joe DiMaggio retired from baseball with a .325 batting average and 361 home runs.

High school and college football, which was played without the now-familiar face guards, was immensely popular. One early superstar was Frank Gifford, who won All–America honors at the University of Southern California before going on to play for the NFL's New York Giants.

A Czechoslovakian athlete named Emil Zátopek stole the show at the 1952 Helsinki Olympics, where he won gold metals in three events: both the 5,000- and 10,000-meter races, as well as the marathon event.

British distance runner Roger Bannister wowed the world when he became the first person to run a mile in less than four minutes. His time? Three minutes, 59.4 seconds.

POP CULTURE

For baby boys, your parents were most likely to name you James, Robert, Michael, John, or David. For baby girls, Mary, Linda, Deborah, Patricia, and Susan were the most popular choices.

That gooey cherub face on Gerber's Baby Food has not changed since your parents were babies. (But the packaging has: your parents ate it out of tin cans rather than jars.)

"Dennis the Menace" first made his way into sixteen American newspapers. The sandy-haired troublemaker proved so popular with suburban parents that, within a year, the comic was printed in one hundred newspapers.

J.D. Salinger published his coming-of-age novel *The Catcher in the Rye* to equal parts acclaim and controversy. By the time you entered high school, reading it was a rite of passage.

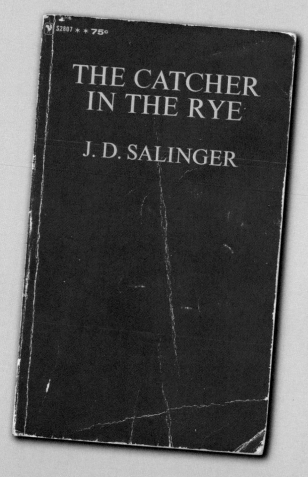

S2807 ** 75¢

THE CATCHER
IN THE RYE

J. D. SALINGER

WHEN YOU WERE
A KID

IN THE NEWS

You can thank Sputnik for all of the math and science you had to take in school. The Soviet launch of the world's first artificial satellite started a space race, and everyone had to do his or her part to ensure American victory.

Many still clung to old prejudices. A Little Rock, Arkansas, high school defied a Supreme Court ruling by preventing nine African–American students from attending their first day of school.

There were only forty-eight states until Alaska and Hawaii became the 49th and 50th in 1959 and 1960, respectively. (But you probably only wanted to vacation in one of them.)

The public assassination of President John F. Kennedy became the defining moment of your generation. For many, it was the end of an era marked by innocence and optimism.

EVENTS

· ·

Your family may have had a fallout shelter in your basement,
for fear of a nuclear attack on American soil. The government
encouraged this precaution, circulating a pamphlet titled
"You Can Survive."

More affluent families had professionally manufactured bomb
shelters installed, such as the Mark I Kidde Kokoon, which
included a three-way portable radio, radiation charts, and a
chemical toilet. (At $3,000, only the exceptionally affluent
had one.)

As the long-term consequences of exposure to even small amounts
of radiation became clear, 9,000 scientists from fifty countries
asked the United Nations to ban above-ground nuclear testing.

The world became a smaller place
with the invention of the jet engine.
Pan American's jet planes offered
America's first commercial trans-
Atlantic flights: New York to London.

Buddy Holly, Ritchie Valens, and JP "The Big Bopper" Richardson met their end in a tragic plane crash.

MUSIC

You probably enjoyed Ross Bagdasarian's Christmas record
"The Chipmunk Song (Christmas Don't Be Late)." Released
under his stage name David Seville, it featured the first appearance
of "Alvin and the Chipmunks."

Some of your other favorite songs might have included
"The Purple People Eater" by Sheb Wooley, "Do-Re-Mi" from
The Sound of Music, and "The Twist" by Chubby Checker.

You heard his music, you saw him on *The Ed Sullivan Show*…
and then Elvis Presley disappeared to spend two years in the Army,
serving first in Texas and then in Germany.

MOVIES

Young explorers were introduced to the mysteries of the aquatic deep through Jacque Cousteau's *The Silent World.*

The New York Times called *Old Yeller* "a warm, appealing little rustic tale," but children of the late '50s will never forget its heart-wrenching climax.

The film's message about racism and the justice system may have gone over your head at the time, but you probably loved *To Kill a Mockingbird* for its young characters and for Gregory Peck's powerful portrayal of Atticus Finch.

TV

There's a reason that you are called "America's TV Generation." 86% of Americans owned at least one television, and the average viewer devoted 42 hours per week watching it.

And why wouldn't you? You had *Lassie, Captain Kangaroo, The Gumby Show, Shirley Temple's Storybook,* and *The Mickey Mouse Club.* You may have lost *Howdy Doody,* but you got *The Flintstones.* (Did you know that the actor who voiced Barney Rubble was Mel Blanc, the voice of Bugs Bunny and his friends?)

If you played "Cowboys and Indians", then you probably also watched *Gunsmoke, Wagon Train, Bonanza, The Lone Ranger,* and *Have Gun—Will Travel.*

Many of the commercials you watched featured catchy jingles that stuck in your head. For instance, you'll probably never forget the tune to Brylcreem's "A little dab'll do ya" advertisements.

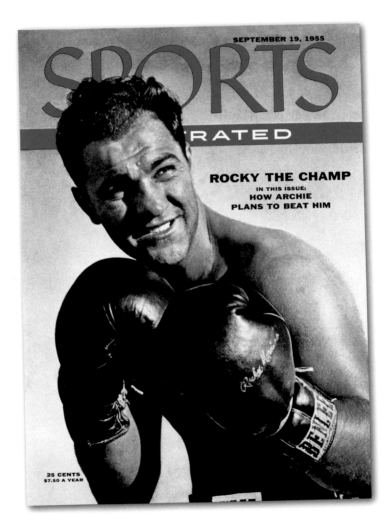

SEPTEMBER 19, 1955

SPORTS

RATED

ROCKY THE CHAMP

IN THIS ISSUE:
**HOW ARCHIE
PLANS TO BEAT HIM**

25 CENTS
$7.50 A YEAR

SPORTS

The only game you may have cared about was the one where you ran around the neighborhood dressed as Davy Crockett or Annie Oakley, but…

…New York baseball fans lost not one but two teams when long-time rivals the New York Giants and the Brooklyn Dodgers both moved to California.

Heavyweight champion Rocky "The Rock" Marciano retired from boxing at the age of 31, undefeated. He won forty-nine fights; all but six of them ended in a KO.

You weren't around when Jackie Robinson broke professional baseball's color barrier by becoming the first African–American to play Major League Baseball since 1889, but you were around when he was the first African–American inducted into the Baseball Hall of Fame.

POP CULTURE

It was a great time to be a kid: new fads such as Hula-hoops, Barbie dolls, Frisbees, Schwinn bicycles, and Davy Crockett coonskin caps all vied for your parents' hard-earned money. Perhaps you were even the proud owner of a Sony TR-63 Pocket-Sized Transistor Radio?

Not everything was new—old classics such as Tinkertoys, Lincoln Logs, and Erector Sets were just as popular during your childhood as in your parents'.

For a special treat (and a night off from cooking for Mom), everyone piled into the family's station wagon for dinner at the nearby drive-in restaurant: perhaps the local Dog n Suds, Sonic, or Sandy's.

Between April and September, the arrival of the Good Humor Man with his crisp white uniform and wide array of frozen confections probably caused a minor riot in your neighborhood.

Hula-hoops, Barbie dolls, Frisbees, Schwinn bicycles, and Davy Crockett coonskin caps all became new fads.

WHEN YOU WERE
A TEENAGER

IN THE NEWS

You mourned the loss of several political and civil rights leaders: Malcolm X, Martin Luther King, Jr., and Robert F. Kennedy were all assassinated within a tumultuous three-year span.

Your late teens were politically fraught—the war seemed without end, there were race riots in many major cities, and the leading Democratic candidate was shot. Richard Nixon was elected for his promise to restore order and for his "secret plan" to end the war.

Whether you served or knew someone who did, you were touched in some way by the war in Vietnam. Nearly 9 million served from 1964–1973, during which time over 58,000 Americans were killed and over 300,000 wounded.

EVENTS

Congress passed the Civil Rights Act, ruling that "discrimination on the basis of sex as well as race in hiring, promoting, and firing" was forbidden. The word "sex" was a last–minute addition, and a monumental victory for the Women's Movement.

In pursuit of his "Great Society," President Lyndon Johnson also passed a series of acts designed to reduce poverty, create affordable housing, protect the environment, provide government health insurance for the sick and elderly, and set standards for the quality of drinking water.

You and one billion other viewers (roughly one-fifth of the entire world's population!) tuned in to watch Neil Armstrong's historic "one small step."

The Eco-Movement, inspired in large part by Rachel Carson's book *Silent Spring*, gained formal recognition by the establishment of Earth Day.

400,000 people attended Woodstock on Max Yasgur's farm in Bethel, New York.

MUSIC

Even if you weren't among the screaming teenagers pelting the "four lads from Liverpool" with jellybeans, you couldn't have missed The Beatles. They already had the top five spots on the Billboard Hot 100 singles chart before their first-ever American appearance on *The Ed Sullivan Show.*

When the unique sound of a Motown hit came on your car radio, you couldn't mistake it for anything else. The Detroit label launched the careers of many black musicians, including The Supremes, whose broad appeal landed them on the top of the Billboard charts twelve times.

Whether you sang along to John Lennon's "Give Peace a Chance," James Brown's "(Say It Loud) I'm Black and I'm Proud," or Creedence Clearwater Revival's "Fortunate Son," revolutionary music both reflected and fueled the times. Perhaps Bob Dylan said it best: "You better start swimming or you'll sink like a stone, for the times they are a-changin.'"

MOVIES

You and your friends probably enjoyed movies about rebels and nonconformists. Of these, Paul Newman's *Cool Hand Luke* gave us the memorable line: "What we've got here is a failure to communicate."

The Graduate, based on the novel by Charles Webb, gave us Simon and Garfunkel's classic song "Mrs. Robinson."

Perhaps you saw 1969's highest grossing film, *The Love Bug,* in a "Herbie" of your own? Drive-in theaters were still popular, and if yours charged admission by the carload rather than per person, they were cheap, too!

There's a good chance that the most memorable movies of your early teenage years were musicals: *My Fair Lady, A Hard Day's Night,* and *Viva Las Vegas* all hit theaters in the same year.

TV

Long before "McDreamy" of *Grey's Anatomy,* you had teen heartthrob Richard Chamberlain as the youthful (and musically inclined) Dr. Kildare.

If you ever said "Sock it to me," "Here come de judge," or "You bet your sweet bippy," then you definitely watched *Rowan & Martin's Laugh-In.*

Walter Cronkite may have changed your mind about the Vietnam War—his unflinching coverage and scathing commentary on the *CBS Evening News* influenced mainstream public opinion.

Other popular shows of your teen years included: *The Beverly Hillbillies, Gomer Pyle, U.S.M.C., Batman, The Andy Griffith Show, Bewitched,* and *The Fugitive* (its final episode was watched by over 25 million households!).

SPORTS

You knew Cassius Clay to be a brash personality who did exactly what he wanted, but many boxing fans were stunned when the world heavyweight champion converted to Islam and changed his name to "Muhammad Ali."

Did you play tennis with a one-handed backhand? Billie Jean King's reign as the top women's tennis player may be responsible for that.

Perhaps you believed that "Winning isn't everything; it's the only thing"? It worked for Vince Lombardi—he coached the Green Bay Packers to a third straight NFL Championship.

New York Yankee Mickey Mantle announced his retirement after a celebrated career that included 536 lifetime home runs and netting American League MVP three times.

POP CULTURE

. . . .

Your first car may have been a brand new Pontiac Firebird, Chevrolet Impala, or Ford Mustang, but more likely, your father gave you his old car—maybe a 1959 Ford Country Squire?

You may have completely horrified your parents by adopting an eclectic Hippy style: peace symbols, long hair, grungy jeans, fringed leather vests, mini skirts with chain belts, granny glasses… Anything goes!

If you were one of 7 million students to enroll in college after high school, you may have found newly opened coed dorms, frequent student protests, and course offerings that included Zen, witchcraft, and Oriental theology.

You may have also joined the growing youth movement to protest American involvement in Vietnam, unequal civil rights, and poverty.

WHEN YOU WERE
IN YOUR 20s

IN THE NEWS

American military involvement in Cambodia, in addition to a new wave of bombing in North Vietnam, prompted those who had remained silent to speak out against the war.

Called in to restore order, the Ohio National Guard fired upon anti-war protestors at Kent State University, injuring nine students and killing four.

Like most Americans, your confidence in the U.S. government was shaken when President Nixon resigned rather than being impeached over the break-in at the Watergate hotel.

You and many others watched, helpless, as Iranian militants seized sixty-six American citizens and held most of them hostage at a U.S. embassy in Tehran for over a year.

Roe v. Wade:

The Supreme Court controversially ruled it unconstitutional to deny women an abortion within the first trimester of pregnancy.

EVENTS

You may have read Betty Friedan's book *The Feminine Mystique* years earlier; if so, you may have also joined the "second-wave feminist" Women's Lib Movement.

Technology seemed to be growing at an unchecked rate: grocery stores started using UPC codes to ring you up, doctors could now see your brain with a CAT scan, and a space station called "Skylab" was orbiting the Earth.

No advancement was as shocking as the announcement of the world's first baby conceived in vitro. The "test-tube baby" was born to Lesley and John Brown, an otherwise average British couple who suddenly found themselves in the center of a media maelstrom.

While the rest of the country suffered from a deep recession, a growing technology boom (not to mention the nice weather) convinced many to relocate to the South and Southwest—these states saw a population increase of more than 25%!

MUSIC

You heard little Michael Jackson
for the first time when Motown
Records released *Diana Ross
Presents The Jackson 5.*

Fascinated or repulsed, it was impossible not to react to your first
sighting of the androgynous space creature with glittery clothing
and orange hair. David Bowie personified "Glam Rock" as Ziggy
Stardust.

You'll never forget the flashing lights, the lit floors... the polyester.
George McCrae's "Rock Your Baby" and the Hues Corporation's
"Rock the Boat" kicked off the short–lived Disco Era.

You lost two childhood icons with the untimely deaths of both
Elvis Presley and John Lennon.

MOVIES

You couldn't look at pea soup the same way again after seeing *The Exorcist*. Arguably the most terrifying horror movie ever made, its grotesque special effects caused heart attacks in some moviegoers.

Science fiction and comic book fans were validated at last by blockbusters like *Superman, Close Encounters of the Third Kind, Alien, Star Trek: The Motion Picture,* and the granddaddy of them all: *Star Wars.*

Whether for pure escapist fun or fear of an uncertain future, disaster movies like *Airport, Earthquake,* and *The Poseidon Adventure* were big hits.

You couldn't argue that John Travolta made disco look good. *Saturday Night Fever* brought the underground craze to everyone's attention, and the soundtrack (which featured several Bee Gees hits) sold 12 million copies.

TV

Your black–and–white television set did not mean that you were completely behind the times—by the early '70s, only half of America watched television in color.

Saturday Night Live premiered, launching the careers of Bill Murray, Chevy Chase, Dan Aykroyd, Steve Martin, and many others.

If you watched anything other than *Roots* between January 23–30, 1977, then you were in the minority. An incredible 85% of the viewing public watched the 12 hour mini-series adaptation of Alex Haley's novel.

After you were inundated with cigarette ads during your childhood and teenage years, the last-ever cigarette commercial was broadcast during *Johnny Carson's Tonight Show,* one minute before new legislation banning them became law.

"We are two wild and crazy guys."

TEVE MARTIN & DAN AYKROYD (AS THE FESTRUNK BROTHERS)

> "I don't want them to forget Ruth; I just want them to remember me!"

HANK AARON

SPORTS

Hank Aaron beat Babe Ruth's home run record of 714 on April 8, 1974. He didn't stop there—Aaron holds a total of 755 career home runs.

Palestinian terrorists held eleven Israeli athletes hostage at the Munich Olympics. With the crisis televised via satellite, much of the world watched in horror as a rescue attempt turned into a bloodbath—all remaining hostages were killed.

Try as you might, you will probably never forget football personality Joe Namath wearing pantyhose for a Hanes Beautymist commercial.

POP CULTURE

By the time you entered the workforce, business attire had become more casual: sweater vests, print shirts, patterned jackets, and ties were the norm.

Your first home probably cost you somewhere in the vicinity of $29,000. (Or you could have snagged the former home of Al Capone in Pine Hill, New Jersey, for $180,000.)

You were most likely to name your children Michael, Jason, Christopher, David, or James if boys; for girls: Jennifer, Amy, Melissa, Heather, or Angela.

You may have joined in on the newest summer craze—string bikinis covered only the bare essentials (and only barely). They retailed for $35–$45.

WHEN YOU WERE
IN YOUR 30s

IN THE NEWS

Whether you voted for him or not, you had to be impressed when President Ronald Reagan returned to work a mere three days after an assassination attempt put a bullet through his lung.

Millions watched in horror as the space shuttle Challenger—whose crew included Christa McAuliffe, a school teacher—exploded moments after takeoff.

No one likes Mondays, but October 19, 1987 was particularly bad: After several months of record gains, the Dow Jones plummeted 508 points—nearly 23% of its total value.

You had to do "duck and cover" drills in school, but your kids wouldn't: The Cold War came to a symbolic end with the fall of the Berlin Wall.

EVENTS

. . . .

Most thought the AIDS epidemic was only a threat to drug addicts and homosexuals until 13-year-old Ryan White made his story known. He had acquired the virus through a blood transfusion.

Perhaps you owned one of the first Apple II computer systems? Soon after its debut, personal computers could be found in many homes. *Time* magazine even revised their "Man of the Year" feature to award the personal computer with "Machine of the Year."

Tired of the looming threat of nuclear disaster, and still shaken by the partial core meltdown at Three Mile Island, over one million people took to the streets of New York City to join the largest anti-nuclear demonstration in history.

Slain civil rights leader Martin Luther King, Jr., was honored with the dedication of a new national holiday, though initially only 27 states observed Martin Luther King, Jr. Day.

MUSIC

Rock 'n' roll had been largely dormant since your teen years, but Michael Jackson revitalized the genre with his sophomore album *Thriller*, which earned Jackson a record eight Grammy awards.

Think the title track to Bruce Springsteen's hit album *Born in the USA* is about American pride? Many did, and still do. However, "The Boss" wrote the song about how shamefully Vietnam veterans were treated after the war ended.

Madonna's self-titled debut album included five hit singles, though the "Material Girl" drew ire for her explicit lyrics and music videos.

Other familiar hit songs include Duran Duran's "Hungry Like The Wolf," Prince's "Party Like It's 1999," and Def Leppard's "Pour Some Sugar On Me."

Sony released the CDP-101—
the world's first CD player.

"I'll be back."

TERMINATOR

MOVIES

You and your kids probably saw *Return of the Jedi, Ghostbusters,* and of course *E.T., The Extra-Terrestrial* in the theater. (You may have left the younger kids at home for *The Terminator.*) Blockbuster popcorn flicks reigned supreme.

Critical hits *She's Gotta Have It* and *Do the Right Thing* lifted young African-American director Spike Lee to prominence.

Tom Cruise became a heartthrob with *Risky Business,* and *Top Gun* inspired a fashion throwback: leather bomber and aviator jackets were popular again.

You may have thought about taking pottery lessons after seeing Patrick Swayze and Demi Moore in *Ghost.*

"Movie night" didn't always mean going to the theater—all you had to do was rent a VHS tape from the local Ritz Video or Movie Gallery and pop it into your VCR. (Just don't forget to rewind!)

TV

You grew up with only three–five channels, but soon there were almost 60! Just a few years after it was introduced, more than half of American homes had cable TV.

With so many more options, how could you possibly watch it all? VCRs to the rescue! Television executives wrung their hands over fear that their audience would simply fast-forward through the commercials.

You may have identified with *Thirtysomething's* Baby Boomers as they navigated the trials of having children and growing older, while *The Cosby Show* was an unparalleled hit with audiences both black and white.

> ## "There's 57 channels and nothing on."

BRUCE SPRINGSTEEN

SPORTS

If it hadn't yet, the widespread cocaine problem in the mid-'80s got your attention when it claimed the lives of two athletes: Len Bias, newly drafted by the Boston Celtics, and professional football player Don Rogers.

The American star of the 1984 Olympic Games in Los Angeles was track-and-field athlete Carl Lewis, who took four gold medals.

Before his illegal betting got him ousted from baseball, Cincinnati Reds batter Pete Rose surpassed 4,191 hits to break a record set 57 years earlier by Ty Cobb.

By 1987, 49.5% of American homes had cable TV. And the most popular cable channel by far? ESPN, with 60 million subscribers by the end of the decade.

Whether you admired her for her speed or her singular fashion sense, Florence Griffith-Joyner (or "Flo-Jo") set records in the 100- and 200-meter dashes at the 1988 Summer Olympics in Seoul, South Korea.

POP CULTURE

Were you a "Yuppie"? It was a good time to be one: young urban professionals saw great profit from the deregulation of big businesses. Many forgot "peace, love, and happiness" in favor of a new credo: "Money is power."

Two instant classics joined the "funnies" section of your newspaper: Gary Larson's "The Far Side" and Bill Watterson's "Calvin and Hobbes."

The private lives of celebrities were suddenly matters of great interest. Supermarket tabloids—such as *Star, The Globe,* and *The National Enquirer*—sold by the tens of millions.

It's all about you! Self-help books, like *You Can Negotiate Anything* and *Be Happy You Are Loved,* began to fly off the shelves.

Trivial Pursuit was the hot new game, plastic flowers danced to music, New Coke was quickly replaced with Coca-Cola Classic, Jane Fonda and Richard Simmons ushered in a fitness craze, and Koosh Balls were loved by children and adults alike.

WHEN YOU WERE
IN YOUR 40s

IN THE NEWS

All fifty-one days televised, the standoff between followers of
David Koresh and federal agents at a Waco, Texas, compound
ended with the deaths of over eighty people.

An eighteen-year manhunt for "The Unabomber" came to an end
when Ted Kaczynski was convicted of killing three people and
injuring twenty-nine more with his homemade mail bombs.

The world was stunned when Princess Diana and her boyfriend,
Dodi Al-Fayed, were killed in a car accident while trying to avoid
paparazzi. A close friend of the Princess, Mother Teresa died of
natural causes only five days later.

Bill Clinton was the first President born
after World War II, and also the first
Democrat to win reelection since 1944.

EVENTS

You may have installed an extra phone line to check e-mail and surf the Web without fear of losing your Internet connection whenever someone needed to use the phone. Full-service programs like America Online offered an easy way to keep in touch and navigate the World Wide Web.

Your science-fiction dreams (or fears) came true when scientists in Scotland successfully cloned a lamb named Dolly, igniting a worldwide debate about the implications of cloning technology.

Just as it seemed you were living in the modern world that had been promised to you as a child, the Y2K bug threatened to send society back to the 1900s by exploiting an oversight in computers' internal clocks.

Genetic modification allowed farmers to begin growing produce that was larger and more resistant to insecticides, though some scientists worried about the effects that these altered crops could have on the environment.

MUSIC

Did your teenagers wear ripped jeans and refuse to comb their hair? They probably listened to "Grunge" bands such as Nirvana and Pearl Jam. Loudly.

Two familiar bands reunited to release best-selling live albums: The Eagles' "Hell Freezes Over" and Fleetwood Mac's "The Dance" both debuted at number one on the charts.

Elton John rewrote an old song and performed it at the funeral of Princess Diana. "Candle in the Wind '97" quickly sold 34 million copies, and all proceeds were donated to charity.

Amidst accusations of sexual misconduct with a minor, Michael Jackson exchanged vows with 27-year-old Lisa Marie Presley.

MOVIES

Moment of truth: How many times did you watch that ship and iceberg collide? Popcorn blockbusters were still king, but new computer technology allowed for special effects on a previously unimagined scale. *Jurassic Park* and *Titanic* paved the way for future CGI spectacles.

Forrest Gump gave a new perspective to the memorable events you experienced and introduced the philosophy "Life is like a box of chocolates."

Everything old was new again. Hit movies based on the television shows of your youth included *The Addams Family*, *The Fugitive*, and *Mission: Impossible*.

You probably also enjoyed *Thelma and Louise*, *The Piano*, and the heartrending *Schindler's List*, which earned a staggering 12 Academy Award nominations and six Oscars, including Best Director and Best Picture.

TV

You may have stayed up late to watch the O.J. Simpson police chase. Every minute of the subsequent trial was also aired live and watched by millions.

Even if you were one of very few people who didn't watch *Seinfeld,* you couldn't escape people quoting it (not that there's anything wrong with that). After nine seasons, more than 30 million people tuned in to watch the series finale.

A former politician and successful news anchor, Jerry Springer became better known as the host of the shockingly disturbing (and wildly popular) *Jerry Springer Show.*

Nearly 60% of Americans spent most evenings on the couch, giving rise to the term "couch potato."

While on that couch, many "potatoes" enjoyed hit shows like *America's Funniest Home Videos, Home Improvement, Ally McBeal, Frasier,* and *ER.*

"Yadda, yadda, yadda."

SEINFELD

SPORTS

Baseball fans were not pleased when a 257–day strike led to the cancellation of 1994's World Series.

After the strike ended, you probably noticed that more people were upset about the high salaries of professional sports players. Michael Jordan, for instance, earned $30 million in one year.

After stumbling in two previous Olympic competitions, American speed skater Dan Jansen exemplified perseverance by taking home the gold medal and setting a new world record in the 1994 Winter Olympics' 1,000-meter event.

Basketball fans were stunned when three-time MVP Earvin "Magic" Johnson announced that he was HIV-positive and would retire from the NBA. However, he later returned to coach his former team, and even came out of retirement to play for the Los Angeles Lakers at the end of their 1995–96 season.

POP CULTURE

You weren't imagining it: Popular culture seemed obsessed with youth as advertisers trained their sights almost exclusively on teenagers. By the late '90s, teens were 31 million strong, and willing to spend most of their money on music and movies.

Dr. Deepak Chopra may have changed your mind about alternative medicine with his best-selling book *Ageless Body, Timeless Mind.* If so, you weren't alone—*Time* magazine even named Chopra one of the Top 100 Icons and Heroes of the Century.

Casual yet durable clothes by L.L.Bean and Eddie Bauer were in, and if your company was one of many that now offered dress-down days, you could even wear them to work!

Fanny packs were hip, emoticons put smiles in your e-mail, Beanie Babies were must-have collectables and books on tape let you read while driving.

> "Men are from Mars, women are from Venus."

AUTHOR JOHN GRAY

IN THE NEWS

President George W. Bush declared war on Iraq, in an effort to find weapons of mass destruction before they could be used against America or its allies.

No one expected the devastation of Hurricane Katrina. The category four storm claimed the lives of nearly two thousand New Orleans natives and the homes of many more.

The space shuttle Columbia unexpectedly disintegrated after its return from a successful 16-day mission. All seven astronauts were killed, and debris from the shuttle rained across hundreds of miles of Texas countryside.

From Mr. Universe to the Terminator to… California's 38th Governor? After surprising the world by announcing his candidacy on *The Tonight Show with Jay Leno*, voters elected Arnold Schwarzenegger over 134 other candidates.

September 11, 2001.
We will never forget.

EVENTS

· ·

From humble beginnings to 44th
President of the United States,
Barack Obama showed the world
that the American dream is very
much alive.

Were you one of 50 million people without power during the
Northeast Blackout of 2003? After a cascading power failure, eight
U.S. states and parts of Canada were left without electricity for a
day or longer.

A massive earthquake measuring 9.0 on the Richter scale loosed
a disastrous tsunami on Southeast Asia, killing over 225,000 and
displacing 1.2 million more.

When you heard the news, you probably thought it was a practical
joke: Pluto is no longer considered a planet.

MUSIC

The world was stunned to learn that Michael Jackson died of a drug overdose less than a month before his series of sold-out concerts in London.

The way you listen to music has changed just as much as the music itself: from LPs to 8-tracks, and then cassette tapes to CDs, and finally to portable MP3 players like the Apple iPod, which can easily hold your entire music library.

With the option to buy your music online by the song or album, digital downloads eclipsed sales of the physical CD. Tower Records, Virgin Records, and hundreds of independent record stores across the country began closing their doors.

American Idol launched the careers of talented performers Kelly Clarkson, Carrie Underwood, Chris Daughtry, and Jennifer Hudson. (As well as musical oddity William Hung.)

MOVIES

. . . .

Echoing in many ways the Eco-Movement of your youth,
Al Gore's *An Inconvenient Truth* raised public awareness
(and debate) over environmental issues.

Academy Award-winning *Dreamgirls* may have seemed familiar
to you—the story closely mirrored that of Diana Ross and
The Supremes.

Marvel superheroes started to find
themselves in successful movies;
Spider-Man, X-Men, and *Iron Man*
were all blockbusters.

Thanks to her powerful performance in *Monster's Ball,* Halle Berry
became the first African–American woman to win an Academy
Award for Best Actress.

TV

Whether you loved or hated it (or loved to hate it), reality television had gained legitimacy. For instance, you may have noticed a new category during the 60th Annual Primetime Emmy Awards: "Outstanding Host for a Reality or Reality-Competition Program."

You may have grown up watching *Candid Camera*, but mega-popular shows such as *Survivor*, *American Idol*, and *The Apprentice* seemed to bear little resemblance to the "Reality TV" of your youth.

Your favorite shows may have gotten the axe before their time. Critically acclaimed shows like *Arrested Development* and *Firefly* were cancelled before many fans had a chance to discover them.

You had to spring for the premium cable package (or wait for the DVDs) to catch some of the most popular shows on television, such as *The Sopranos, Six Feet Under, Battlestar Galactica, The Wire,* and *The Shield.*

"You're fired!"

DONALD TRUMP

SPORTS

Long-beleaguered Boston Red Sox fans had their day when their team beat the St. Louis Cardinals to win their first World Series Championship in 86 years.

NASCAR fans were stunned when seven-time Winston Cup champion Dale Earnhardt suffered a fatal crash during the final lap of the Daytona 500.

American cyclist Lance Armstrong has survived cancer and taken home seven Tour de France titles—and counting!

American swimmer Michael Phelps won eight events at the 2008 Beijing Olympics, setting a new record for the most gold medals won in a single Olympics.

POP CULTURE

You have likely discovered the Internet phenomenon that is YouTube—endless hours of homemade hilarity, and some other things you wish you could forget.

Even if you never cared much for video games, you probably couldn't resist the Nintendo Wii. (Just don't forget to fasten that strap around your wrist! Your television will thank you.)

Perhaps you wondered why celebrities your age started looking younger than you do? In many cases, the answer was Botox injections, which temporarily paralyze certain facial muscles, smoothing wrinkles and creating a more youthful (if somewhat puffy) face.

If your children had children of their own, your grandson(s) might be named Jacob, Michael, Matthew, Joshua, or Christopher. Your granddaughter(s) might be named Emily, Hannah, Alexis, Ashley, or Sarah.

Facebook:

A new way to keep in touch, even with people
you haven't seen since high school.

MOST PEOPLE YOUR AGE ARE:

- Married, with at least some college education.
- Homeowners and employed.
- Living in California, Texas, New York, Florida, or Pennsylvania.
- Enjoying a higher household income than any other age group.
- Worried about keeping pace with the cost of living.
- In better health than the generation before.
- Driving (or hoping to buy) a BMW, Lexus, Infiniti, or hybrid.
- Looking forward to retiring in five years!

LOOK WHO ELSE IS IN THEIR 60S:

. . . .

- Peter Agre, biologist
- Jeff Bridges, actor
- Sven-Goran Eriksson, English football coach
- George Foreman, boxer
- Whoopi Goldberg, actress/talk show host
- Al Gore, American politician
- Bruce Jenner, athlete
- Donna Karan, fashion designer
- Jessica Lange, actress
- Jay Leno, talk show host
- Bill Murray, actor
- Gloria Naylor, novelist
- Ozzy Osbourne, singer/reality TV star
- Nora Roberts, author
- Mark Spitz, athlete
- Bruce Springsteen, singer/songwriter
- Cat Stevens, musician
- Stevie Wonder, singer/songwriter

IF YOU HAVE ENJOYED THIS BOOK
WE WOULD LOVE TO HEAR FROM YOU.

Please send your comments to:
Hallmark Book Feedback
P.O. Box 419034
Mail Drop 215
Kansas City, MO 64141

Or e-mail us at:
booknotes@hallmark.com